I CAN DO IT · 2

WORKING WITH PAPER

Written and illustrated by
HOWARD MELL & ERIC FISHER

SCHOFIELD & SIMS LTD · HUDDERSFIELD

7217 4501 6
First Printed March 1968

Printed in Great Britain by
W. S. Cowell Ltd at the Butter Market, Ipswich

Contents

A Word of Advice

You will find that you can enjoy making the things in this book much more if you remember some simple rules:

Before you begin: always cover your desk with newspaper. Put out the things you need.

When you are working: do not let things get too messy.

When you have finished: clean the things you have used and put them away. Put scraps in the wastepaper basket.

Keep things tidy – including yourself!

4

1. *Using Strips of Paper*

This is a book about things we can make from paper and card.

We use paper for all kinds of things – for drawing, writing, painting.

What else do we use paper for?

If you look around the room you will see all sorts of things made with paper.

This book, for example, is printed on paper.

Then we use paper to make bus tickets, paper bags, handkerchiefs, toilet rolls, wallpaper.

We even use paper to make money.

Have you any paper money of your own?

What other things can you think of that are made of paper? Make a list.

You could start with writing paper, drawing paper, greaseproof paper (the kind butchers have), corrugated paper (do you know what that is?).

Now add some more kinds of paper to your list.

We shall be using all kinds of paper to make the things in this book.

And what about card? We use it for birthday cards, soap and cornflake packets, tickets and cardboard boxes.

Some card is nearly as thin as paper, some is so thick you need a saw to cut it. We shall be using paper and card that you can cut with scissors or a knife.

The things on your list are probably made from different kinds of paper. How many different kinds do you know?

Here are some of the other tools we shall need besides scissors and knife:

1. A stapler.

2. Drawing pins and ordinary pins.

3. Paper fasteners. These have two prongs. You make a hole in the two pieces of paper you wish to fasten. Then you push the paper fastener through and open the prongs at the other side, as the drawing shows.

4. Glue. Rubber pastes like Copydex and the sort of rubber solution used for mending bicycle punctures are best.

5. Sellotape and paper tape (usually brown) which has glue on one side.

6. A pencil, a ruler, a rubber, and some compasses for making circles.

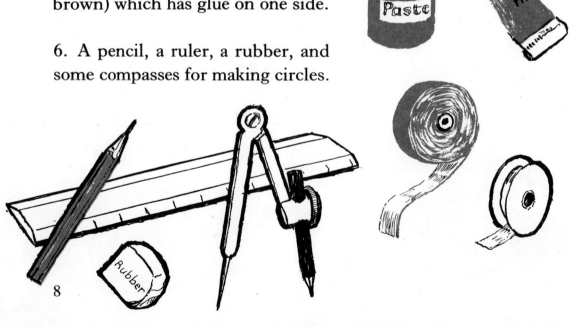

A hanging lantern

Shall we start by making some very easy things with strips of paper?

You will need :
 Pencil, ruler, scissors, stapler and one or two cornflake packets.

Cut some strips from the cornflake packet. This is the easiest way to do it: Put your ruler down. Draw a line at each side of it. Then cut along your lines.

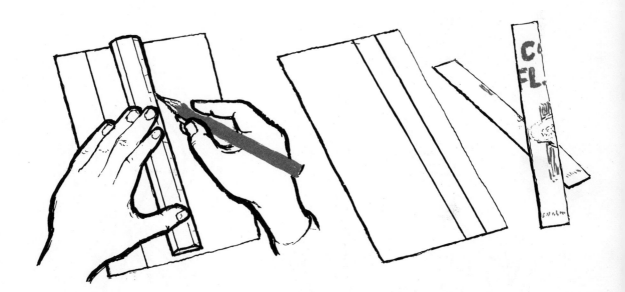

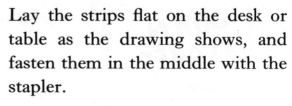

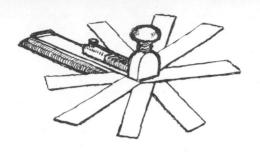

Lay the strips flat on the desk or table as the drawing shows, and fasten them in the middle with the stapler.

Now bring up the other ends together and staple them as the drawing shows.

You have made a sort of ball. You can put other strips in if you like.

Perhaps you would like to stuff some coloured tissue paper into the space in the middle, before you staple the last strip down.

Try making balls with *coloured* strips. Can you make balls of different sizes?

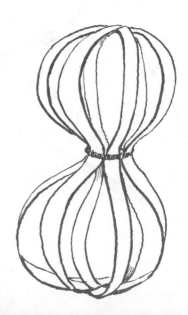

A fish

This is made very easily from one strip of card.

You will need :
    Scissors, a cornflake packet or other thin card and some paper handkerchiefs, or coloured tissue paper or paper towels.

Cut a strip of card and make slits in it half way across, near each end, as the drawing shows. Now bring the two slits together and push them into each other and you have a loop of card, shaped like a fish.

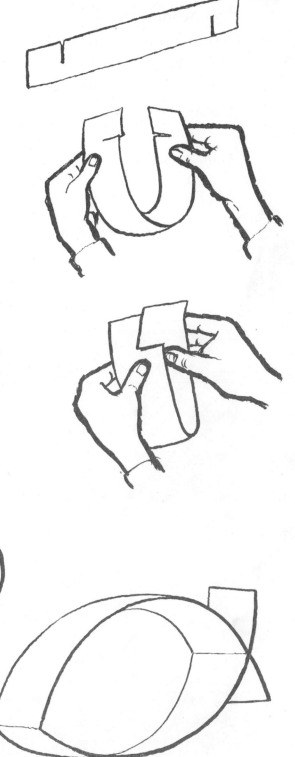

By pushing and squeezing, and nipping the mouth end, you can alter the shape. Push in a paper handkerchief or towel, or coloured tissue to fill in the body.

Can you fill in the body in other ways?

The picture shows one filled with a coloured strip.

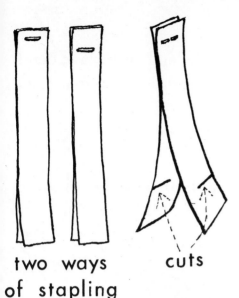

two ways
of stapling

cuts

A bird

For this you will need :
    Paper, scissors, staple machine,
    paper tissue or paper towel.
Cut two strips of paper.

Staple them together at one end.
This will be the beak of the bird.
Near the other end cut slits half way
across, as the drawing shows.

Fit the two slits together and you
have a simple bird shape. Push
some coloured tissue paper – or a
paper handkerchief – or a paper
towel into the loop. This fills in the
body. Or you could use strips to
make the body as the other drawing
shows.

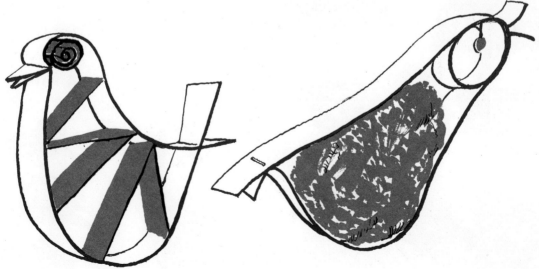

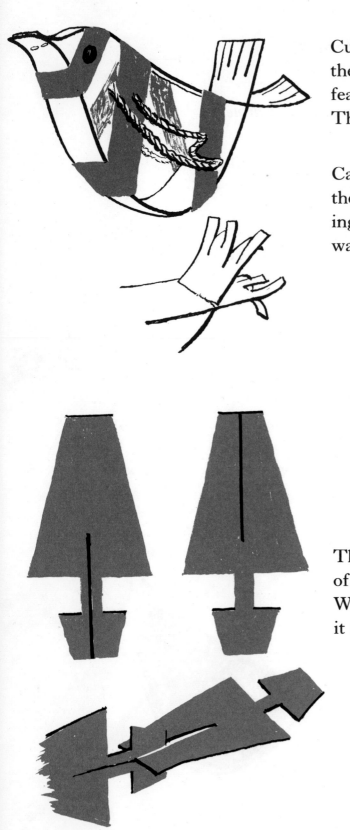

Cut slits in the end of the tail; bend the ends up and down to make tail feathers.

The drawing shows you how.

Can you add other things to make the fish and the bird more interesting? What else can you make in this way?

This tree was made from two pieces of card. Each piece has a slit in it. When the slits were pushed together it stood up like this.

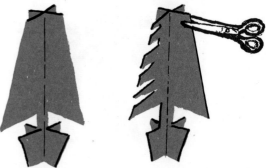

A curled paper pattern

Here is another thing which you can make very easily, using strips of paper.

You will need some light coloured paper (white or yellow) cut into strips. The strips should be not more than one foot long and one inch wide. You will also need a piece of dark coloured paper (black, brown, or blue). About 12 inches by 10 inches would be a good size. This is the background paper – we shall stick our strips on to it.

And you will need scissors, thick paste or rubber "cow-gum" and a ruler.

First, we need to curl the strips.

Do you know how to curl paper?
Let me show you how. There are a
few ways.

1. OVER RULER OR SCISSORS

Hold one of your strips in one hand.
Now hold your ruler in your other
hand as if it were a sword.

Slide the piece of paper between
the ruler and your thumb and pull
it through.

What has happened to the paper? It
should have made a long curl.

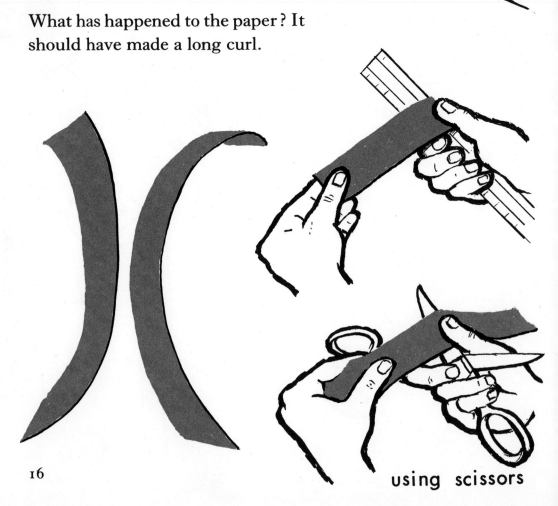

using scissors

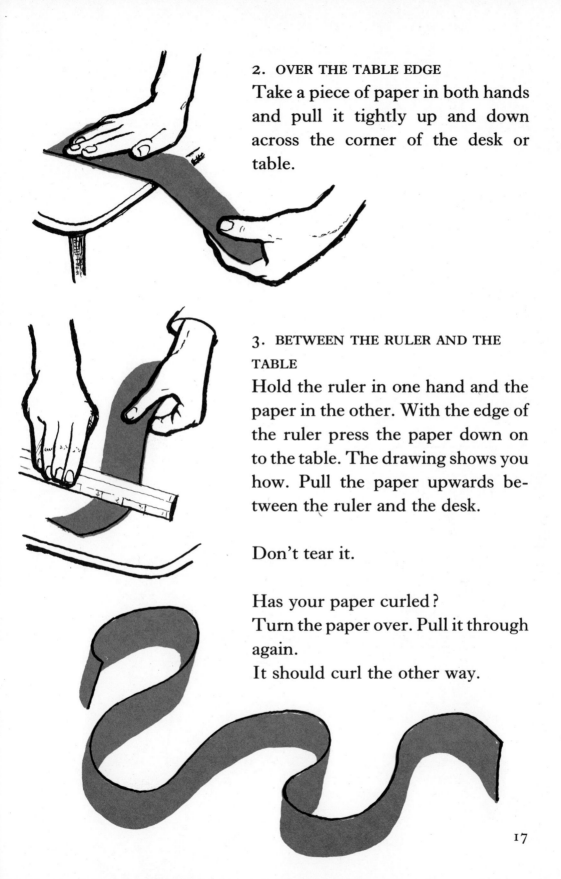

2. OVER THE TABLE EDGE

Take a piece of paper in both hands and pull it tightly up and down across the corner of the desk or table.

3. BETWEEN THE RULER AND THE TABLE

Hold the ruler in one hand and the paper in the other. With the edge of the ruler press the paper down on to the table. The drawing shows you how. Pull the paper upwards between the ruler and the desk.

Don't tear it.

Has your paper curled?
Turn the paper over. Pull it through again.
It should curl the other way.

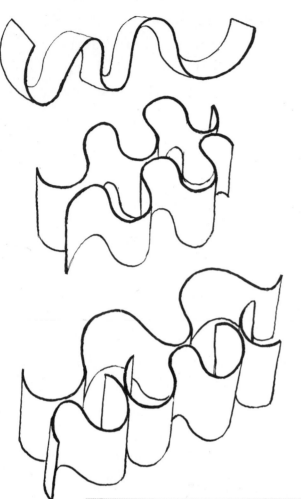

This wavy shape is made by pulling it through like this. First one side up and then the other.

Make some curly shapes that you like, arrange them in a pattern standing on their edges. The drawing at the bottom shows how they look on the background paper.

Don't stick them down yet.

Do you like the pattern you have made?

If you moved the curly pieces about could you make a better pattern?

When you are pleased with your pattern take up some paste on a paste brush or even on your finger.

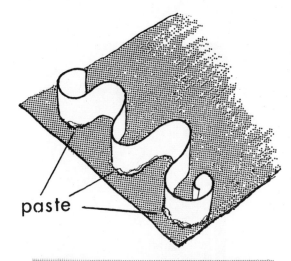

paste

Paste a little along the edge of each curly strip. Set it down on the background paper where you want it to go and press it gently.

Do the same with all your other strips in the pattern. Give the paste a little time to set. This is the pattern I made. It looks a bit like wrought iron.

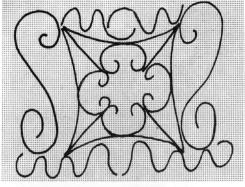

Do you know what wrought iron is? Perhaps you pass a wrought iron gate on your way home.

Making a paper tree by curling

Cut the corner from an oblong piece of paper.

The pictures will help you with this.

Cut slits in the slanting (left hand) side and stop about an inch from the other side. Later you can try shorter slits.

Put a pencil in the bottom end and roll it up. Roll the paper round the pencil.

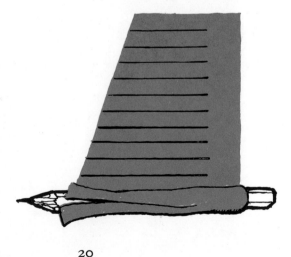

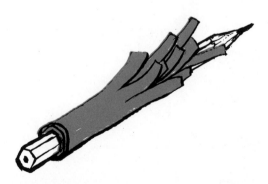

Stick some sticky tape round the
bottom end.

Slide the pencil out.

Now curl the slit pieces between a
ruler and your thumb. Curl carefully, don't pull the pieces off!

What does yours look like when you
have finished?
Mine looked like a palm tree.

Making a paper chain and a paper star

The chain and star in the drawing were made from strips of paper.

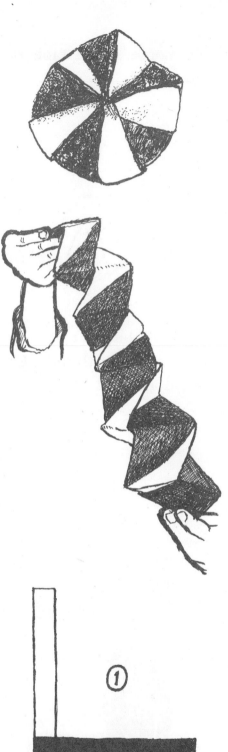

Let's make the chain first. After that it will be easy to make the star.

You will need :
Scissors and stapler and two long thin strips of paper – one black and one white. About two feet long and two inches wide would be good.

Put the two strips on the table in front of you so that they make a big letter L with the white strip going away from you.

Staple them at the corner with the black one on top. Drawing 1.

Fold the white strip forward towards you over the end of the black one. It looks like Drawing 2.

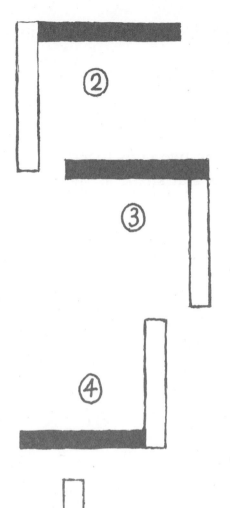

Fold the black one from right to left. Drawing 3.

Fold the white strip away from you again. Drawing 4.

Fold the black one back from left to right. (Drawing 5.) It looks like a letter L again but a lot smaller, because we have folded some of the paper. Keep on folding. When you come to the end, cut off any spare bits. Staple the black and white ends together.

If you hold it in both hands it looks like this.

Bring the two ends together and it makes a star shape as the drawing shows.

What happens if you use other colours of paper?
Two wider strips, or two narrower strips?
Or one narrow and one wide strip?

Before you go on, here is a puzzle using strips

You will need :
   Paper, newspaper will do, glue and scissors.

Cut some strips at least two feet long and about two inches wide.

Put one of the strips on edge on the desk and mark the ends as the drawing shows: so that 1 is behind 3 at one end, 2 is behind 4 at the other end.

Bring the two ends together, making a ring, so that 4 goes on 3 and 1 and 2 are showing. Paste the ends together.

What do you notice about your ring? It should have one twist in it, like the one in picture B.

What do you think will happen if you cut the strip lengthways down the middle? Picture C shows you how. Now cut it. Go right round.

What happened? Do you have two rings, or what?

Take another strip. This time, join the ends together making two twists – see the drawing D.
Cut down the middle again.
What has happened this time?

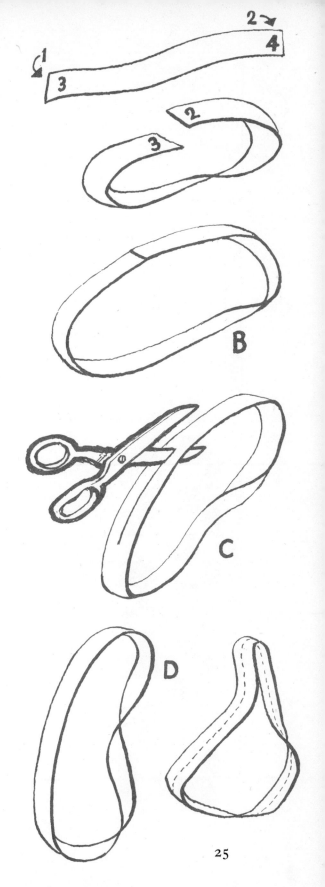

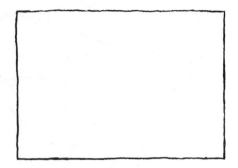

Weaving with strips of paper

You will need :

Scissors and two colours of paper.

In one piece of paper cut some slits as the drawing shows.

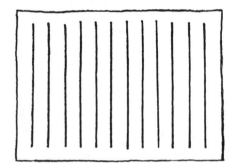

From paper of the second colour cut some strips. Weave them in and out through the slits, over and under. The drawings show you how. You will think of all kinds of patterns to make.

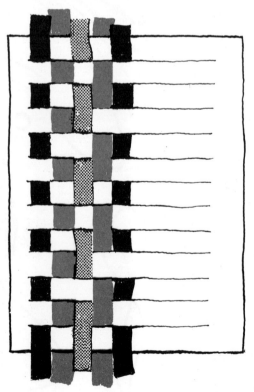

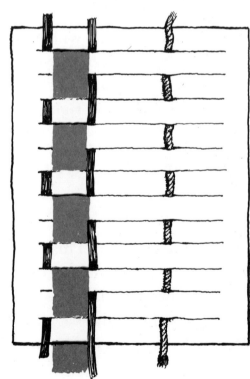

If your background paper (the piece with the slits in it) is dark, then your strips should be light. Then they will show up against each other.

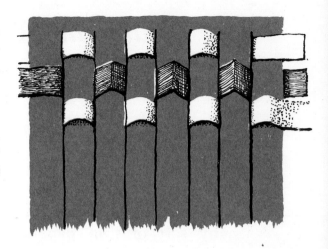

Here is another pattern which I made. I pushed strips through the slits. What is different about it?

Can you make one like this?

2. Folding and Cutting

Making cut paper patterns

You will need :
   Scissors and paper.
Any sort of thin paper will do.
Typing paper, writing paper, even
kitchen paper. You may have some
coloured paper; perhaps you should
save it until you have had a little
practice with the plain paper.

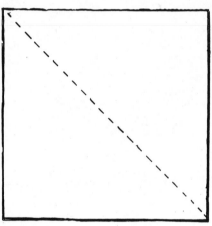

Spread some newspaper on the desk
to catch the bits of paper which will
drop out when you cut.

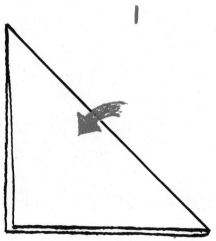

Start with a square of paper like
picture 1. 8 inches by 8 inches is a
good size but any size which you
can hold easily will do. Fold the
square across the corners, putting
one corner on the opposite corner.

Press the paper flat.
Picture 2 shows you how.

Fold it again, bringing the top
corner (a) to the bottom corner (b).
Now you have a shape like the one
in picture 3.

Put it on the desk with the longest
side at the bottom. Fold the side in
two, putting one corner on top of
the other (picture 4).

Now you have a smaller triangle!

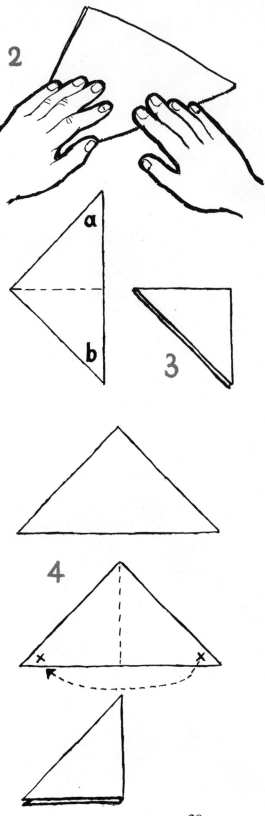

Cut some pieces from any side of the triangle.

Which cuts are easiest to make — straight ones or curved ones? You can make good curving cuts by holding the scissors still in your right hand and moving the paper.

The picture shows you how. Don't be afraid, cut out big pieces as well as little ones. When you think you have cut enough, open out the paper. What does it look like? Are there still some big spaces with nothing cut out? Would you like to cut some more out? Can you make a better pattern?

Fold the paper again and cut more away. Try as many ways as you can. Remember to cut away plenty of paper.

When you have finished cutting, spread your patterns out on a background which shows them well. Black or coloured paper would be good if your cutting paper was white.

What could you do to make your patterns better?

There are lots of other ways of folding the paper, can you think of some?
Your teacher might help.

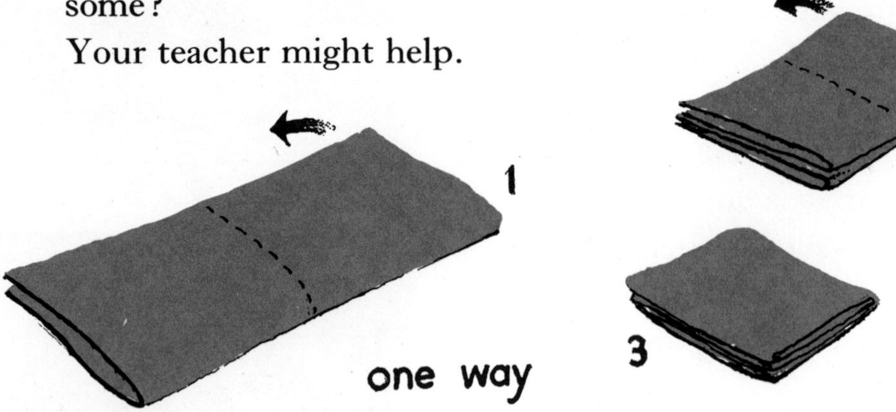

one way

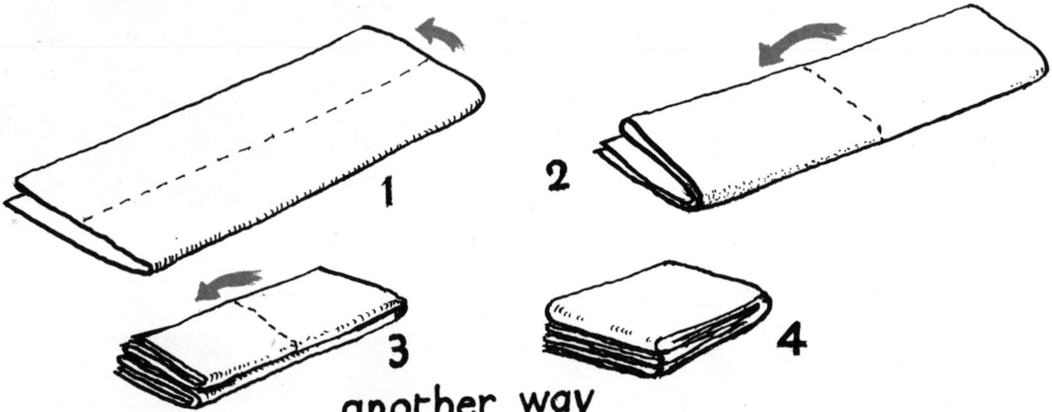

1

2

3

another way

1

2

3

4

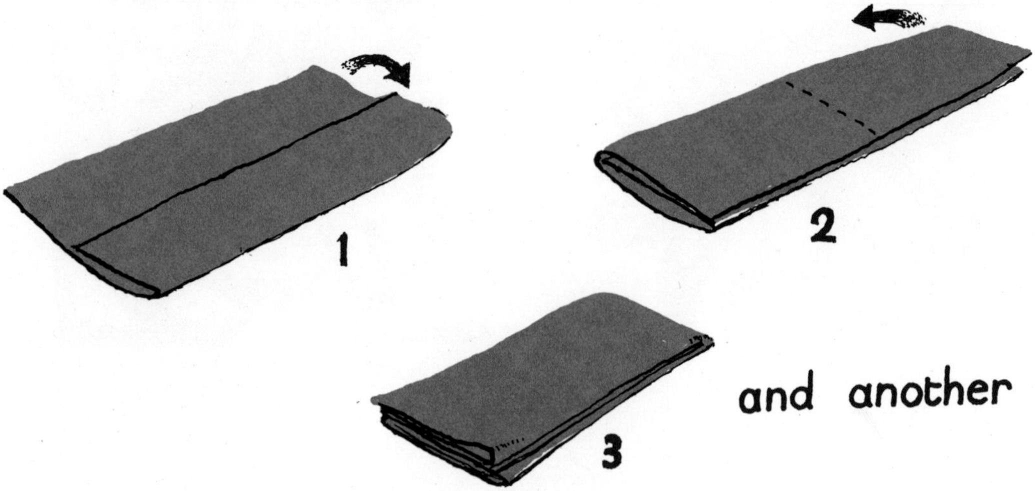

and another

1

2

3

How to stick your patterns on to a background – this is known as "mounting".

Put your pattern on a piece of paper and set it to one side. Now choose the paper that you are going to mount your patterns on.

Paste the mounting paper – not your cut-out pattern. Bring your cut-out pattern to the pasted mounting paper and slide it gently off, onto the mounting paper. Press your pattern down gently.

Making a chain of figures

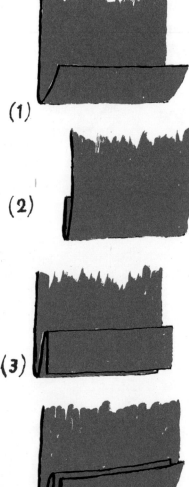

You will need :
A long strip of fairly thin paper – typing paper or kitchen paper, and some scissors.

(1) Fold up about an inch at the bottom, press the paper flat. Now turn the paper over (2). Fold back again as this picture shows (3). Turn over again (4) and fold back.

Go on turning over and folding until you reach the other end; now your paper looks like picture 5. This is called a concertina fold (do you know what a concertina is?).

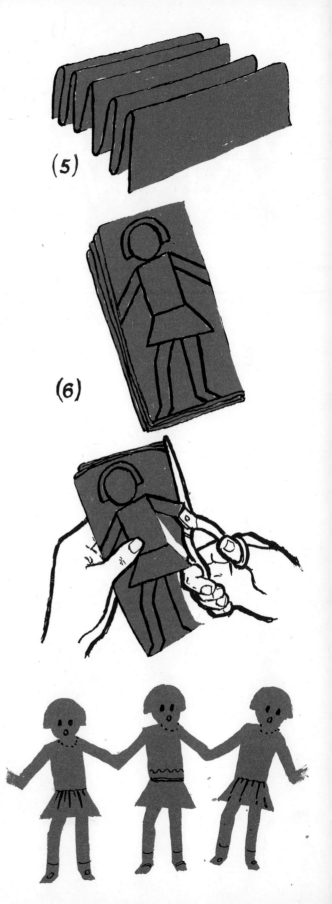

(5)

Fold the whole packet together and draw a child on the top (6). The child can be standing or dancing, wearing a cap or not, as you like, but the hands must go out over the edge. Why is that? Now cut out the figure.

(6)

If the folds of paper are too thick, and it hurts your fingers to cut all at once, try cutting a few at a time.

When you have cut out the figure, open up the paper. How many children have you in your chain? Are they holding hands? How can you make eyes, noses, mouths on the children?

Paste a piece of coloured paper — wallpaper will do. Put on plenty of paste. Stick your cut-out people onto this. If you wish, you can slide some of the legs and arms up or down, before the paste dries.

36

We can use the concertina folds for other things too.

Making a star

You will need :

    A piece of paper, a stapler and scissors.

Take a strip of paper. This strip must be at least ten times as long as it is wide. How long will your strip have to be if it is 2 inches wide?

Fold it in a concertina fold. Fasten it in the middle with a stapler. Don't draw on it this time but cut some pieces out of the folds – just as you did for the cut paper patterns on page 30.

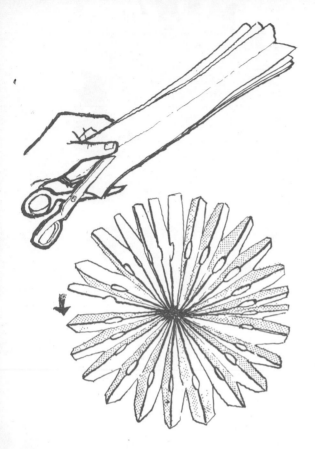

If the folds of paper are too thick and the scissors hurt your fingers, let a few folds go, and cut them later. The picture shows you how. Then open out each side like a fan and join the ends together with a paper clip – or stapler or glue.

Do you like your star? What else could you make with concertina folds? You might make this bird.

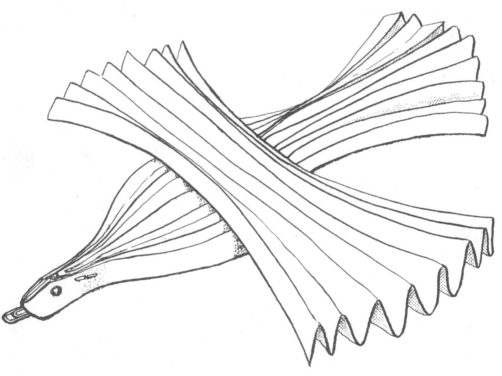

38

3. *Masks and Hats*

Do you like wearing masks? Would you like to make one?
Here are masks which are quite easy to make.

For the main part of the mask you will need scissors, stapler, Sellotape, one large sheet of paper or thin card and some other smaller pieces to make hair, nose, eyes, etc.

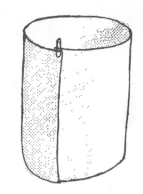

Bend the paper or card to make a big roll.
Fasten the ends with paper clips.

Does the roll slide down over your head?
Make it fit by making the roll wider or narrower.

If you like you can cut some pieces out so that the mask fits over the shoulders. Look at the top of page 41.

When it fits, mark the paper to show how far it has to overlap.

Paste the ends together or fasten them with the stapler.

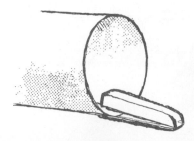

Now that you have the main shape you can add curled paper for hair, eyes, nose, moustache, beard or whatever you like.

The nose can be a curl of paper sticking out at the front, or you can make the nose in one piece with the eyes if you like. The pictures here show you how.

You will think of lots of other ways for decorating your mask, perhaps using coloured tissue or string or raffia or buttons.

There are some other good shapes for masks.
Here is one.

You need scissors, paper or card, stapler and Sellotape as before.
Cut the piece of paper or card so that it covers your face. Now fasten string or elastic to the edges to hold the mask on.

To do this make a hole an inch from the edge, thread your string or elastic through and tie a knot. You could make it stronger by putting Sellotape over the place where the string goes through the hole. You can cut slits in the top as the drawing shows.

Bend the cut pieces forward to make a fringe, or make slits at the bottom and bend them upwards to make a beard.

You can make your mask still better by cutting two slits in from the corners (a) and (b) as the drawing shows.

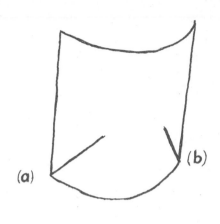

Bring the sides of the slit together and overlap them as the drawing shows. Staple or paste the two together.

Do the same at the other side.

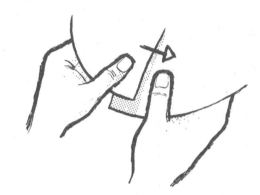

Now cut the bottom to the shape of a chin. If you wish you can do the same at the top. Cut some slits, overlap them and shape the forehead like the chin.

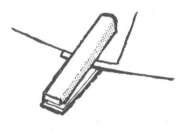

Now go on and add things to finish your mask.

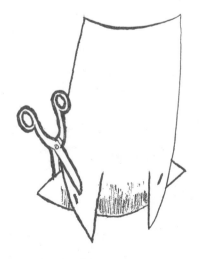

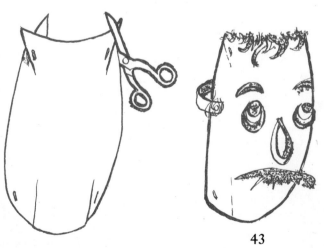

Here is another way of shaping paper for a mask.

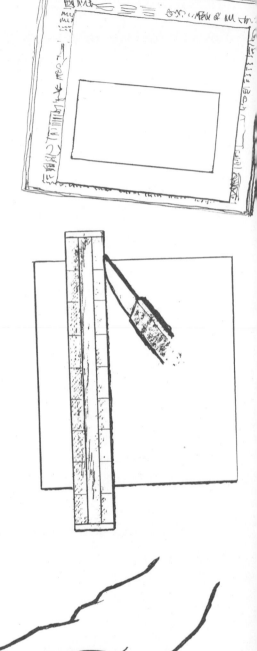

You will need :

    As before, a large sheet of paper or thin card, some scrap card to cut on, scissors, Sellotape or gummed paper tape, stapler and ruler.

One of the best ways to make the paper bend is by scoring – I don't mean scoring a goal. When we score paper we make a groove or line in it. Let's practise on a spare bit of paper first.

Put the paper flat on the desk or table on some layers of newspaper or a sheet of spare card. With scissors, a knife or the end of a ruler press a groove or line on it. Start with a straight line using a ruler. Next, try a curved line.

If you can't draw a smooth curve get a tin or a hoop and draw round that. When you make your scored line don't press too hard or you will cut right through the paper.

Now pick up the paper and bend it along the scored line you have made. Always bend the paper away from the scored line, the drawing shows what I mean.

That wasn't very hard was it?

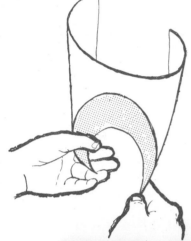

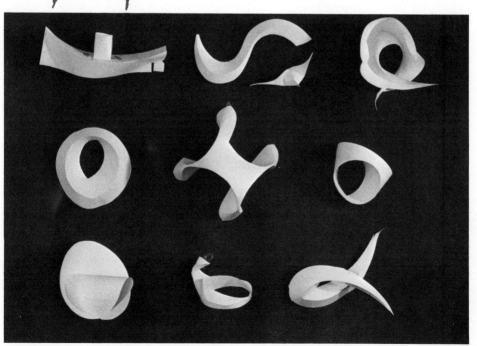

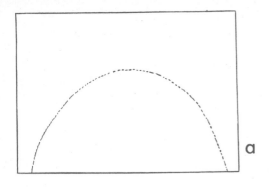

a

Making another mask

Now we have had a practice let us use scoring to bend paper for a mask.

Make your scored line as the drawing (a) shows, then bend the paper. It will make a shape something like the drawing (b).

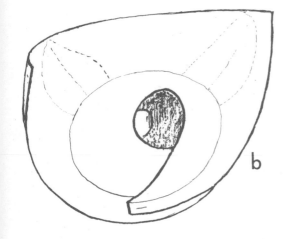

b

Does it make you think of an animal's head?

You could make a mask from a cone of paper as the drawing at the bottom of this page shows.

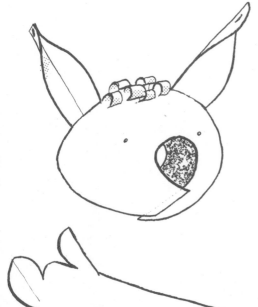

Take hold of a sheet of paper by corners x and y and look at the pictures on page 47.

Now bring your two hands together and let the two corners overlap. Staple or stick them together and you have a cone.

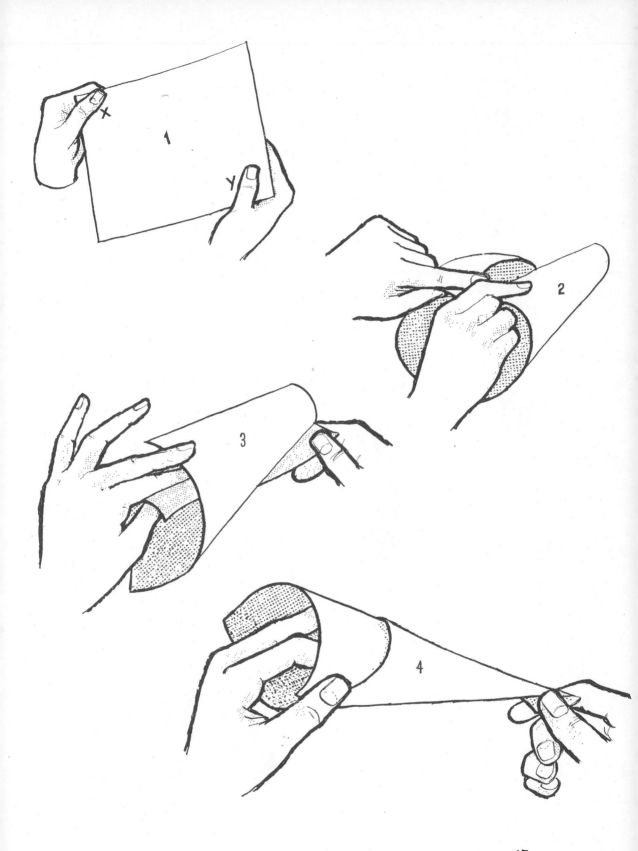

Making a paper hat

You will need :

Scissors, a knife, stapler, Sello-tape or gummed paper tape, a large sheet of paper and some smaller pieces.

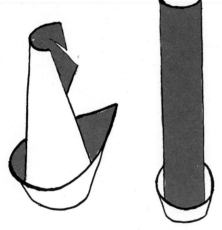

This hat shape is made by scoring the paper as you did for the mask. Begin in exactly the same way. Make a scored line either freehand or with a hoop.

Bend the paper, and it forms this sort of shape.

Some nuns have white hats just like the one on the left. Have you seen them?

You can cut off some of the brim or edge of your hat if you wish, or you could make some slits in the edge and curl the pieces.

Look at the hat on page 48.

Can you see how many things I have put on it? Do you recognize them? You can make them all from this book. For example, the long chain which runs from top to bottom is shown on pages 22 and 23. What else can you think of?

You could decorate it with tissue paper. I am sure you will think of all sorts of things to fasten on.

Another hat

You will need :
   Scissors, stapler, Sellotape or
   gummed paper tape, and this time
   a pair of compasses and a pencil.

With your compasses draw two
circles from the same centre, a big
one and a smaller one. The drawing
shows how. Score the smaller circle.

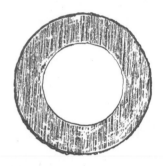

The space between, which is the
shaded part in the drawing, will be
the brim of the hat. You can make
it wide or narrow, as you wish.

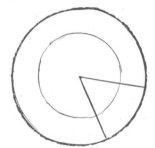

Cut out a wedge like a piece of cake.
Now bring the two edges together,
and let them overlap a little. Turn
up the brim. Glue or staple the
edges. There you have a hat with a
turned up brim.

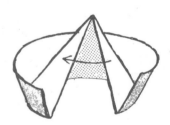

By drawing another circle you can
turn the brim down as the bottom
drawing shows.

Look what I have done to the brim of my hat. Can you see how it was done?

What can you think of to do to yours?

What can you add or stick on to make it different?

4. Lanterns,

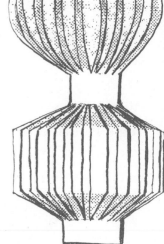

Crowns

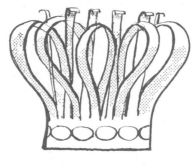

and things

Have you ever made a paper lantern like the one on the right?

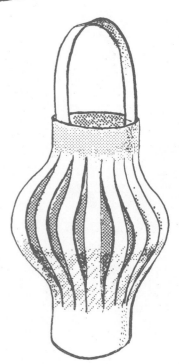

You will need :
Some (two or three) sheets of paper, drawing paper or sugar paper or a sheet from a wallpaper pattern book would do. Scissors, glue (rubber paste), stapler, paper clips and Sellotape would be useful but you can do without them.

Cut slits in your paper like the ones in the drawing, leaving margins top and bottom. (For a piece of paper 20 inches by 10 inches the margins would be about 2 inches.)

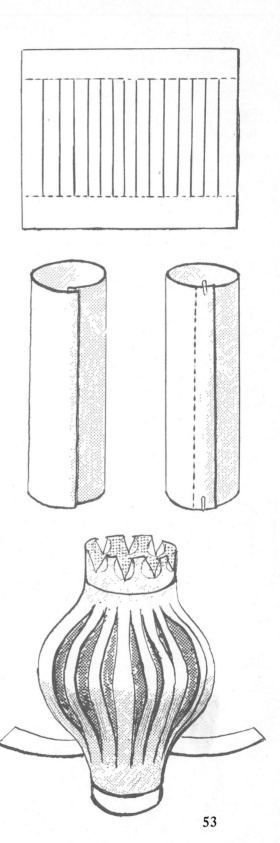

Take another piece of paper and make a simple tube by pasting the short ends together. Put a paper clip over the join to hold the paper until the glue sets. The drawing shows you how. This shape is called a cylinder.

Now take the first piece of paper — the one we cut slits in — and wrap it round the tube or cylinder and paste it or staple it. If some of the cylinder sticks out at the top you can cut it off or cut parts of it off to make a pattern.

Cut a strip of paper and stick it on as a handle if you wish.

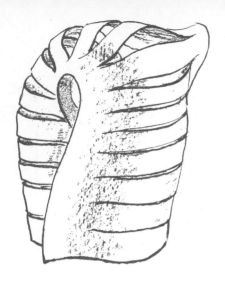

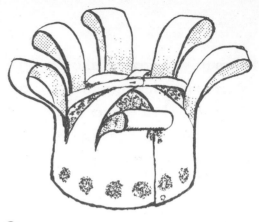

Crowns

Would you like to make something else? We can make a lot of interesting things using paper which has the same sort of slits in it.
Shall we try?

You will need :
The same things as before: paper, scissors, stapler, glue, paper clips.

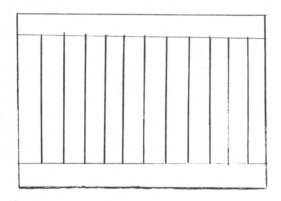

Take a piece of paper and cut slits in it as you did for the lantern. The drawing shows you how.

Now bring the top edge down to the bottom edge and paste or staple them together. Put paper clips on to hold the paper until the paste sets.

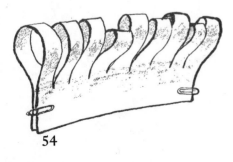

54

Now bring the two end loops together and you have a shape something like a crown.

Does yours look like a crown?

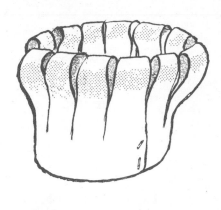

What does it look like if you bend one loop outward, the next inward and so on – mine looked like the drawing a.

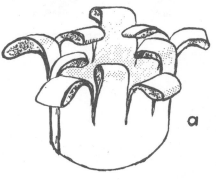

a

What other shapes can you think of?

All the shapes on this page were done from this beginning. Try some for yourself.

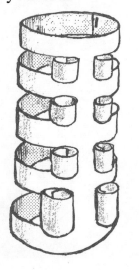

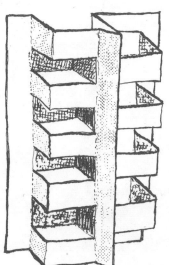

This tree is made by slitting and folding the paper as on page 54. Then instead of making a crown, wrap the paper round a pencil and curl it as on page 21.

Look at the pictures at the bottom. One of these shapes was made by bringing the opposite corners of the oblong together. Others were made by cutting and curling some of the strips.

ALL of them were made from paper cut in slits.

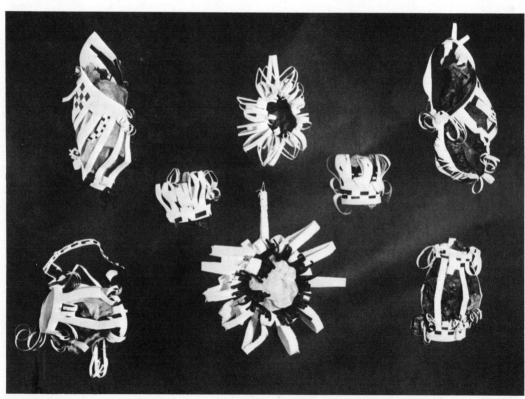

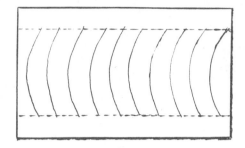

What happens if you cut curved or zigzag slits?
Try it and see.

What other kinds of slits and cuts and curls and joins can you think of?

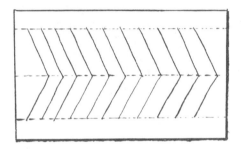

When you have finished, put all your shapes together and see which you like the best.

Perhaps you would like to join some of them together to make a big lantern.

5. *Paper Animals*

Up to now we have made stars, masks, etc., but we can use paper to make models of all these things as well.

You will need :

Fairly stiff paper (perhaps from a wallpaper pattern book) or thin card (old birthday cards or calendars), some scissors, and a pencil or ballpoint pen to draw with.

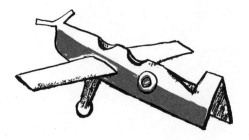

First, let us make a simple dog. Take an oblong piece of paper or card and fold it in half lengthways.

Draw the dog on the paper with his tail, his back and his head along the fold. Notice that you need draw only two legs. The drawings show you how.

Now cut along the line which you have drawn.

Does your dog stand up?

What other animals can you make?

Your teacher will tell you how to make the aeroplane and the tree on page 58.

Look at this giraffe. The little drawing shows the folded paper he was cut from.

The dotted line shows where to put the feet.

Can you make one?

59

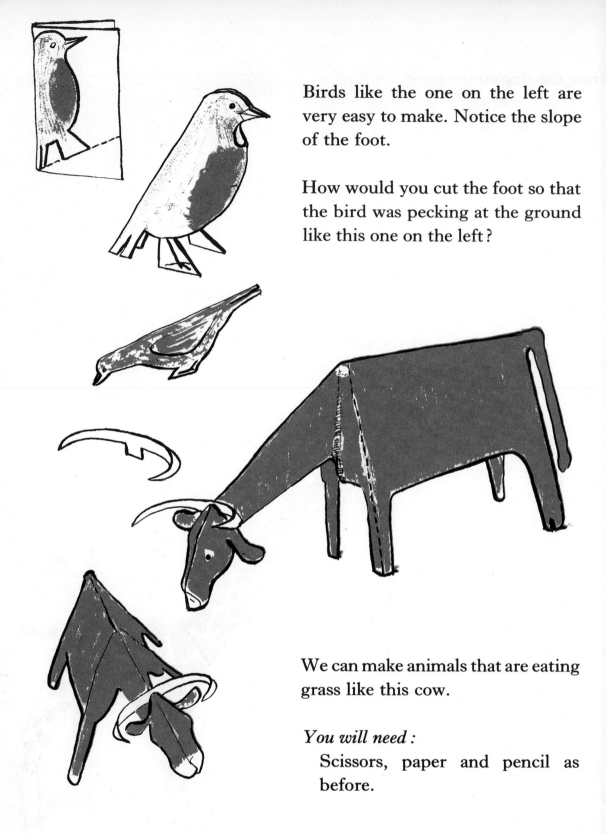

Birds like the one on the left are very easy to make. Notice the slope of the foot.

How would you cut the foot so that the bird was pecking at the ground like this one on the left?

We can make animals that are eating grass like this cow.

You will need :
 Scissors, paper and pencil as before.

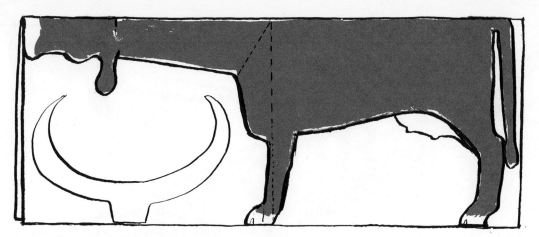

Take your paper and draw your animal, cow or sheep or horse, but this time give him an extra long neck. Cut the horns out separately and stick them on later.

Now when you fold the animal, nip the neck part in one hand. Hold the body part in the other hand but not so tightly.

Press the neck part downwards and backwards and it will fold into the body part. The drawing shows how.

Try it. It is easier to do than you think.

Can you fold the neck upwards? This horse has his head up. The little drawing shows you what the folds look like.

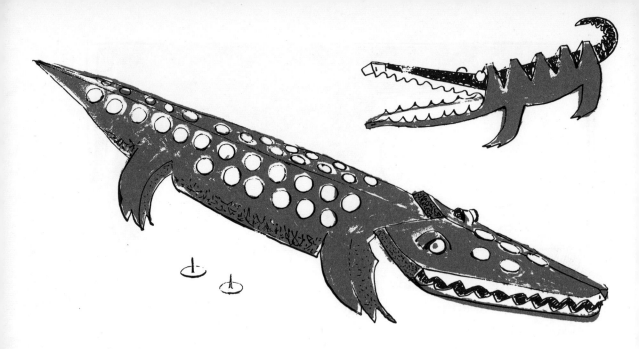

Now let's make an animal with a broader back.

You will need :
    Paper, pencil, scissors, as before, and this time a ruler.

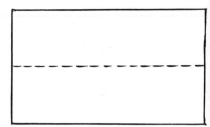

Use the ruler to draw a line across the middle of the paper. Now draw two more lines, one on each side about an inch from the centre line.

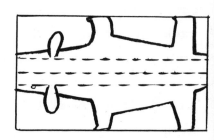

Next draw the animal you would like to make. The drawing shows how.

Cut it out, bend along the lines and stand up the animal on its four legs.

Here are three more creatures made in the same way, can you make them? What else can you make in this way?

Can you see how this bridge and the bus were made? They are quite easy really.

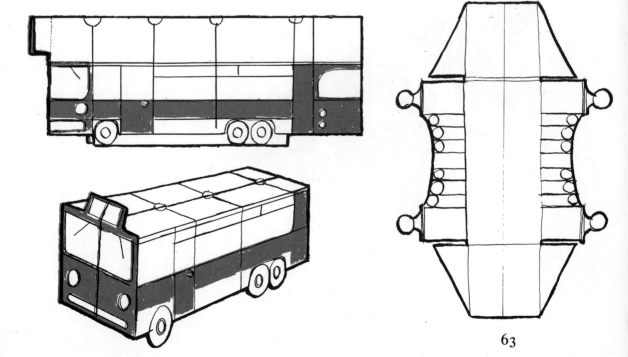

You can of course paint your folded paper models. Some children like to print patterns on the paper with potato. This is hard to do once the paper has been folded and stood up.

If you want to do it, paint the pattern whilst the piece of paper is still lying flat on the desk. Or you can stick tissue paper and other things on to give your animal a furry coat or a shiny coat. Try your own ideas. Find out what happens.

Here is an animal made this way.

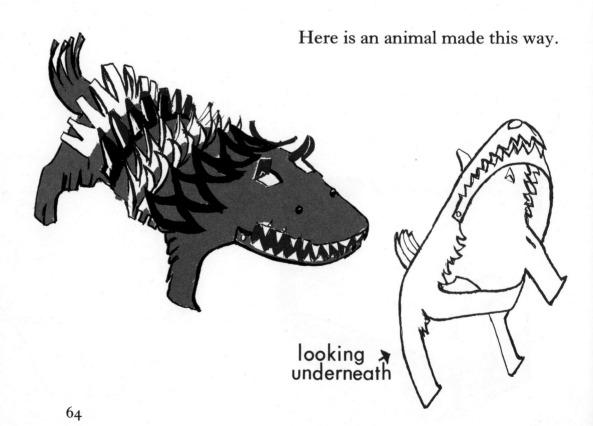

looking
underneath

Not all your folded paper models have to stand up. You can hang them from a light or from a line across the classroom if your teacher will allow it.

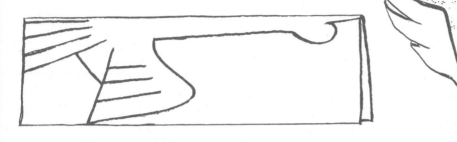

This bird seems to be flying. What else do you notice about it? Yes, he has had the edges of his wings and tail cut with slits and then curled.

What else can you make in this way? Discuss it with your teacher.

You can also make animals from tubes and cones of paper.

You will need :
   Scissors, paper, paste, stapler, pencil or ballpoint pen.

Make a tube or cylinder of paper – like the one in the drawing – by rolling the paper. Sometimes a tin might help, roll the paper round it.

Paste the edges together. This is the body of your animal.

Now make four more tubes, thinner ones, for the legs, then one for the neck and one for the head.

You can make these thinner tubes by rolling the paper round a pencil, or use drinking straws.

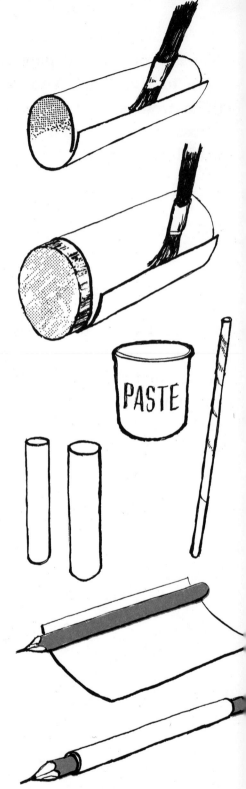

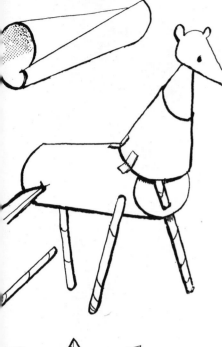

The neck and head need to taper, that is they should be narrower at one end than at the other as the drawing shows.

You can make paper tubes do this by overlapping the paper more at one end than the other.

Fasten the legs and neck to the body by pushing holes into the body with your ballpoint or scissors. Then push the legs in through the holes. The neck is fastened on in the same way.

If you make two-legged things — like birds — use blobs of plasticine for the feet and stick the legs into them.

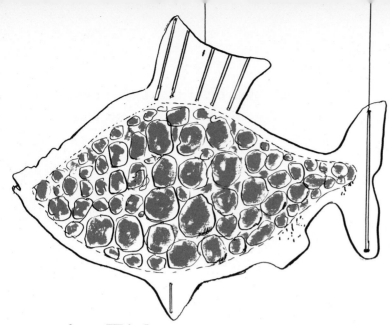

6. Fishes and Birds

Here are some more things that you can hang in your classroom. They are very easily made. Let's make the fish.

You will need :

Scissors; rubber paste or Sello-tape; a stapler; some coloured paper, the kind of paper you can see through which you find in boxes of chocolates or biscuits. Some cellophane, polythene, tracing paper or other paper that you can see through.

(Polythene is not paper, of course; but it is very good for this fish model because it is clear – you can see through it.)

Take 2 sheets of your transparent paper or polythene and put them down flat, one on top of the other on the desk. Now draw with crayon, or felt pen or paint the fish (or bird or whatever you want to make).
Then cut round your lines, cutting both sheets at once so that you have two flat sheets the same shape.

Next, staple, or stick, or tape the two pieces together round the edges – not all the way round, but leaving a hole.

Into the hole push your bits of coloured tissue paper to fill the inside. Then finish joining the edges. Do you like what you have made? Do the colours show through from the inside?

Can you think of more decoration? Perhaps fins or scales fastened on the outside.

Try making other things in this way.

7. *Things which move*

Have you seen windmills like these before?
They spin on sticks.
They are very easy to make.

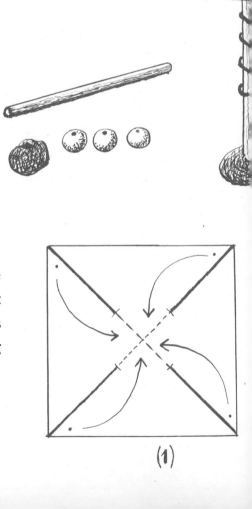

You will need :

1. A square of paper – drawing paper or stiff wall-paper.
2. Scissors.
3. A pin or a piece of thin wire.
4. A pencil or a stick.
5. A lump of plasticine.
6. 2 or 3 beads with holes through. You can make the windmill without these beads, but the beads make it spin better.

Take your square of paper and fold it diagonally, that is from corner to corner. Cut along each diagonal from the corners to about $\frac{3}{4}$ of the way to the centre as in the drawing.

Take each corner in turn (where the dots are in drawing (1)) and take it to the centre so that the four points overlap in the middle. The drawing here shows how.

(1)

Push a pin through all four points and through the back and push the point of the pin into a stick or pencil behind. It should spin when you blow on it. Does yours?

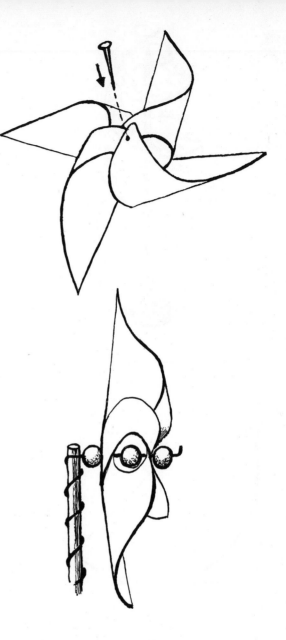

Sometimes the windmills spin better if, instead of a pin, you pass a thin wire through a bead, then through the paper windmill, then through another bead.
Twist the rest of the wire round a pencil or stick. The drawing shows you how.

When your windmill is made and spins well, try putting spots of colour on each corner.

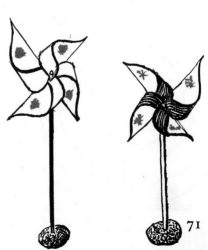

What happens to the colour when the windmill turns?

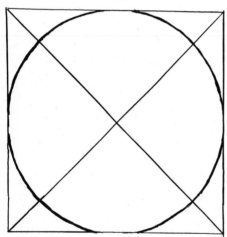

A spinning spiral

Another paper shape which will move in the air is the spinning spiral.

For this you will need :
A piece of stiff paper or thin card about three inches square (an old birthday card or Christmas card would be good), scissors, a knitting needle or a ballpoint pen. A lump of clay, or plasticine or a matchbox.

First make a circle on your card with compasses or by drawing round a cup or lid. Then draw a line like the one shown in the drawing and cut out along your line.

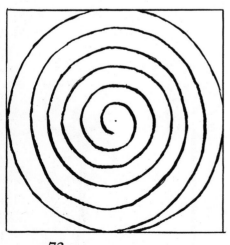

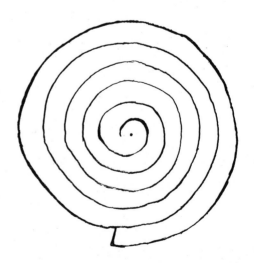

Using your ballpoint pen press a little dent or dimple in the centre of your cut out shape. Look at the drawing here.

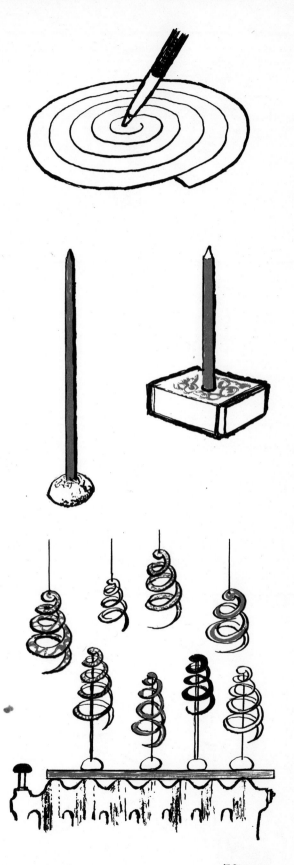

Stand your knitting needle, pencil or ballpoint pen point upwards in a lump of clay or plasticine or in a matchbox.

Put it on a radiator or over something which has warm air rising from it — but not an open fire or anything which might be dangerous. Ask your teacher about this.

Now sit the centre of your cut out piece of card on the point of the needle or ballpoint.

It should turn round and round. Does yours?

Why does it spin like that? If you hang it from a string over a radiator it will also spin.

8. Stretching Paper

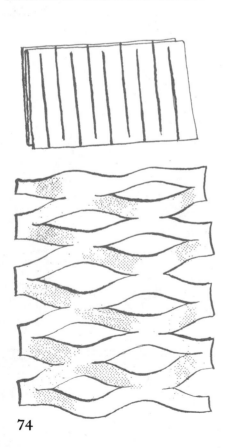

You will need :
    Sheets of thin paper (typing paper or kitchen paper will do), scissors.

Fold your paper in three. You can do this by measuring. If the paper is 9 inches wide, each fold will be 3 inches wide. Or you can do it by eye, guessing the width.

Now cut slits first from one side then the other as the drawing shows. When you have finished the slits unfold the paper. Hold each end and pull gently and it should look like this.

You can make some more stretched paper designs using a different number of folds. Use three, five and seven folds for example. Can you make them?

Here are some other things you can try.

Making a paper net

This lovely net was made in the same way.

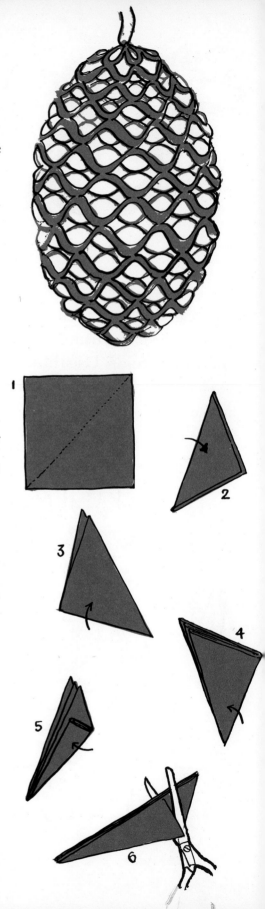

You will need :
A square of thin paper, kitchen paper or newsprint, or coloured paper about the same thickness, scissors, string, a balloon to go inside.

Start with a square of paper (drawing 1). Fold the paper in half diagonally so that the edges meet exactly (drawing 2).

Then fold it again (drawing 3) and then again (drawing 4).
Fold once again (drawing 5). Cut off the end pieces as in drawing 6.

Now cut slits first from one side and then from the other, almost, but not quite, to the other side. The lines on the drawing at the top of the next page show you how.

Unfold the paper carefully – it will break if you are clumsy – until you have a large disc or circle of paper on the desk with slits in it. Look at the drawing.

Take a piece of string and fasten it to one of the outside loops. Then go round the circle, gathering the outside loops on to your string. The drawing shows you how.

Lift it up and pull the middle down gently. You now have the net which we saw at the beginning. You can put a balloon inside and blow it up.

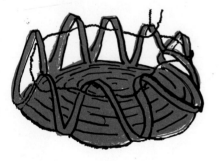

You can make other nets by cutting curved lines, or by cutting the paper when it is folded like the drawings at the bottom.

I hope you have enjoyed all the different ways of making things from paper.

Perhaps you would like to make some of them again.

You will make them better next time.

When you have made all the things in this book you will be able to make all sorts of other things. They could be for plays and parties or just for fun.

How many different things can you make?

Index